"CAKE IS LOVE AND LUST IS FROSTING. CHERISH EVEY BITE"

INSATIABLE SEDUCTIONS

IS

Copyright © 2019 by Cortez Maurell Lewis
All rights reserved. This book or any portion thereof
may not be reproduced or used in any manner whatsoever
without the express written permission of the publisher
except for the use of brief quotations in a book review.

Printed in the United States of America

First Printing, 2019

ISBN 978-0-9973294-2-1

Wordman Times Publishing
THE POETRY PROVIDER

This book in its entirety is a compilation of poems, thoughts, and views of Cortez Maurell Lewis. This body of work is includes prior & never released passion poems. Built on romance & crafted by seduction, this book is designed to lead you on a provocative path of sensuality and happiness.
May it guide you well

CONTENTS:

Hot Chocolate…………...p.1

She Is Amnesia…………...p.4

Wild Thing………...6

All The Time………...9

I Beat The Lovers Drum pt. 1………12

I Breathe Lust And Hope For Love…..14

Oh My Bedroom………...17

Scent Of A Bubble Bath………...20

Mz. Pretty Feet…………...23

This Moment Right Now………26

Arousal Is In The Air………...29

The Wolf And The Woo………...32

A Special Kind Of Kiss………...35

CONTENTS:

Step Inside…………..37

Wink At Me…………..40

Empress Of Seduction………..43

Stunned To Enchantment………..46

Cinnamon Sweat…………..50

Her Genes In Blue Jeans………52

She Knows It…………..55

Egyptian Honey………..58

Tiger Of Love……………..61

Dance For Me……………..64

Thoughtless Feelings………..67

El-Oh-Vee-E…………..70

Grey Space…………..73

CONTENTS:

The Colors Of Attraction.........76

Pounce..............80

I Beat The Lovers Drum pt. 2.........84

BONUS CONTENT:

*Familiar Faces In Places
  (A letter, about a story)**..........86**

*Provocative Affirmations
  (repeat these to yourself)**.........91**

Insatiable Seductions...........

HOT CHOCOLATE

HOT CHOCOLATE

Black butterscotch, caramel coconut in a cup. Cookies-n-cream, brown sugar with a vanilla scent of lust. Let me spin my straw in you and watch the waves swirl through. With a thick blast of honey almond, it's a hot chocolate whirlpool.
So hot the heat could melt marshmallows and make our bodies feel warm. I could feel the temperature level rising in your soft steamy form. When I get you on the table or on the countertop, you're a simply delicious delight from your bottom to your top,
down to the last drop,
I just don't want to stop.

Hot chocolate....hot chocolate....
So many flavors to savor. After
every time I finish, you keep me
coming back later. Addicted to
sweet sips by the touch of the
tongue, I believe that I need you,
hot chocolate got me sprung!!!

SHE

IS

AMNESIA

SHE IS AMNESIA

Who is she?
I like to call her amnesia.
I forget everything I know
at that moment when I see her.
The colors she wears on her
body, makes me want to touch
her so tender. No need to
capture my soul,
it's ready to surrender.

Who am I....? Who am I....?
I don't know... I don't know...
I see her walk by.
I don't want her to go.
I can't remember my name,
I have forgotten where I'm at.
And at that very moment,
my brain is kidnapped.

WILD THING

WILD THING

You're a wild thing
With a wild smile & stare
You have a wild style
And a headful of wild hair

You like fast cars
And high heels
Long trips
And expensive meals

You play real innocent
In front your own crowd
You are a quiet freak
But you moan loud

You're in the fast lane
You live the life
You can fill a man's void
But you can't be a wife

Because half of you is a tease
The other half is temptation
You only live for the thrill
Of satisfying sensations

Can't be tamed or held down
You're a free-spirited friend
It's a pleasure to be with you
Then you're gone with the wind

You're a wild thing

ALL THE TIME

ALL THE TIME

I think about you
I think about you
All the time baby
I think about you

All these songs
Go through my mind
When I listen to the music
You run through my mind

I want to hold hands
And go for walk
I want to laugh and joke
And have serious talks

I want to hang out with you
And have all types of fun
From adventures and parties
To all the foods that are yum

We could start in the house
Then venture the world outside
For crazy places to make love
And sneaky ways you can ride

Whether exhilarating quickies
Or all the foreplay stages
I'm turned on just picturing
You make intimate sex faces

Climax climax
Every moment is surreal
No matter what we are doing
Every moment is a thrill

I think about you
I think about you
All the time baby
I think about you

I BEAT THE LOVERS DRUM

I BEAT THE LOVERS DRUM...VOL 1

I HEAR A RHYTHM

I FEEL A VIBRATION

I HEAR WHISPERS

I FEEL A SENSATION

I HEAR AN EMOTION

I FEEL A BODY CONVERSATION

MY HANDS MOVE WITH PASSION

I BEAT THE LOVERS DRUM....

I BREATHE LUST AND HOPE FOR LOVE

I BREATHE LUST AND HOPE FOR LOVE

I feel the sun shining on me.
I smell flowers. I see a peach.
I'm running through the sand
along the shore on the beach.
This is how I feel inside

I hope love is in reach.

I can hear the wind blow.
It whispers in my ear.
Touch the future it will glow.
Is the beautiful breeze I hear.
This is how I feel inside

I hope love is near

Now I'm moving in a trance,
hypnotized by a glance.

When I ponder positions of romance, you take my breath away and leave me with a hyperventilating pant.
This is how I feel inside

I hope love gives me a chance.

OH MY BEDROOM

OH MY BEDROOM

It's the playground of love, satisfaction you can trust. Nothing feels the way it does, when you and I become us. Your body yells romance, breathing deep on every syllable. I'm moving like a slow jam, in every spot that I'm kissing you. Sweat dripping from our bodies, as if we are standing in the rain. I put pressure on your passion, you get pleasure out the pain. It's hot in here, it's dark in here, the music is playing to our groove. The thundering & lightning outside, looks like sparks are flying in our room. If these walls could talk, they would say two things.

We are moving up & down like elevators, and back & forth like time machines. It's wonderful, it's paradise, all day and all night. You really don't have to say a word. The bedroom knows what you like....

Oh my bedroom..!!

SCENT OF A BUBBLE BATH

SCENT OF A BUBBLE BATH

When you walked up, you had the scent of a bubble bath.
I could even picture the soap and water running down your back. Your skin is so soft, you make the word flesh sound sexy. It feels like I'm breathing your body heat when you stand next to me. You always look so fresh and clean; your perfume reminds me of baby powder.
I want to kiss you gently on your naval, down to your patch of lady flowers. Last night
I dreamed about you.
Before I slept, I thought of you steadily. I'm confused, my conscious tells me its lust, emotions tell me it's destiny.

You can be my lover, or you can
be just a friend to me. We could
just wave hi walking by,
or we could exchange energy.
No matter the situation, when
I'm around you, happiness
grabs me. And every time
I say your name,
my tongue tastes like candy.

MZ. PRETTY FEET

MZ. PRETTY FEET

Your pretty feet float by like
you're walking on air.
The ground turns to sugar as
you step from here to there.
The sexy colors
you wear on your nails,
are beautiful like stripes on
rainbows. With French tips,
it looks like frosting dripping
off the tip your toes.

You look good in those
high heels with the laces.

You look good in those
sandals and ankle bracelet.

You look good in those
flipflops, or barefoot naked.

Your movement is so attractive,
with every step that you take.
Your skin tone glows, like
honey in a sunny place.
A magical work of art,
soft for the eyes to see.
A treasure map of seduction,
that starts at your pretty feet.

THIS MOMENT RIGHT NOW

THIS MOMENT RIGHT NOW

Right now, I keep thinking
about all of this. Whatever
space I have in my mind,
you are taking up most of it. So,
I'm going for this walk, Hoping,
to walk you out of my memory.
Looking to latch on to anything
in my vicinity.
Something else to think about.
Something else to fill my cup.
I would dump it out myself, but
I'm not the one who filled it up.
You did... oh you did...
You did it with your presence.
You magnetized to my eyes,
as I clung to your essence.
Now here comes your aura
chanting provocative hints,

now I'm eager for the flavor
of your provocative scent.
I wish I could forget it.
I'll forget you soon, I hope.
The quicker I forget you,
The quicker I can cope.

AROUSAL IS IN THE AIR

AROUSAL IS IN THE AIR

I noticed a scented aroma, then
I heard a song play. So I
followed my thoughts down the
hallway. I see candles in a dark
room, giving off light with
continuous change. As it was
dimly lit by the flicker,
of slow dancing flames.
Shadows cascade across the
walls as the two bodies moved,
frolicking and teasing half-
dressed and half nude. On top
of a plush burgundy bed, with
laced pillows and satin sheets.
The sounds of urges and
moaning grew, as if they're
reaching their peaks.
I ask myself why I'm here
witnessing what I see.

Wait... As I look closer at the two, I realize one is me. Hold on a minute how could this be, and who is that women nestled under me. As I rush in closer, to see what this means. I start to wake up from some type of daydream. I was standing in line drifting off in a daze. Then I noticed a woman looking at me, as if she was dreaming the same!

Arousal in the air...

THE WOLF AND THE WOO

THE WOLF & THE WOO

It's hot outside in the night,
waiting for that midnight
summertime breeze.
Streetlights make shiny objects
sparkle and her skin illuminate
in the dark like glowing things.
I feel like a magician. Maybe,
this is a magical situation.
I hope I can go with the flow
and use her heart as
transportation.
I could be patient like a wolf,
scoping under the moonlight.
Howling in anticipation, of the
next time she moves by.
Emotions and attractions
can be the call of the wild,
like predator and prey when
the heart chases a smile.

When the eyes connect,
unleashing the courtships of
primal vigor. I'm moving with
carnal instinct, in pursuit of her
enticing figure.

Maybe
it's the nature of passion.
Maybe
it's just passion in nature.

In the hunt for satisfaction, we
all display intense behavior.

A SPECIAL KIND OF KISS

A SPECIAL KIND OF KISS

I wish I could live this moment
twice, 3 times,
4 times, forever again.

Standing under the moonlight
I wonder, will this be my
soulmate, lover, or friend.

A thunderstorm of feelings
aroused by this kiss,
a combination of all things
bountiful and bliss. Again, our
lips touch, making the sounds
of sensual heat.
Embraced in each other's arms
we become complete.
Our thoughts are connecting,
and our bodies crave more.
Heavily breathing anticipation
of what we have in store.

STEP INSIDE

STEP INSIDE

I step into your space
with erotic sentiments.
Hug and embrace you until
it starts to feel intimate.

Pick you up off your feet and
throw you on top of the bed.
Then stare into your eyes,
visualizing what's ahead.

Pin you down into submission,
seductively hold you in place.
Then you lock your legs around
me, closing your thighs
on my waist.

I sink my mouth into your neck,
biting down with
a caressing tongue.
As you squirm in pleasure
letting wild thoughts run.

You can hear me breathe
as the kiss moves towards
your ear. Then down over
your shoulders, as your breast
become near.

I bounce my lips softly down
your stomach, until I'm parallel
to your hips. Plunge my face
between your legs,
with a gentle hungry kiss.

We began exchanging long
climaxes and thrilling rides.
To the doorstep of fantasy,
and then we step inside.

WINK

AT

ME

WINK AT ME

I'm feeling some feelings, and that's indisputable. Just like the nervous butterflies you get, from something seductive & unusual.

Wink at me.. Wink at me..

Show me you feel the same way. Show me the feeling is mutual and we're on the same page. Do you want it like I do? Your eyes say that you need to. Honestly, I've been mesmerized from the moment I first seen you. There is something between us, your wink is recognition. Your smile is conformation, that your wishes are my wishes.

I'm an open book of love, turn the page and read my mind. Then wink at me with your heart, if your thoughts are just like mine.

Wink at me....

EMPRESS OF SEDUCTION

EMPRESS OF SEDUCTION

What species are you?
What planet are you from?
I never seen anyone like you.
You make my heart run.

Racing to its own beat,
as if it jumped out my chest.
Feline... oh feline... the purr
from under your dress.

You have special powers to
control and manipulate minds.
Your enchanting beauty is truly
one of a kind.
Your aura is very compelling,
and your attraction powers
are intensely magnetic.
Your body is built perfect,
with heavenly genetics.

Your presence is like candy.
The eyes are subdued
by its beckon. You're the
empress of seduction, and
sexuality is your weapon.

STUNNED

TO

ENCHANTMET

STUNNED TO ENCHANTMENT

I'm a prisoner of your presence,
you have the beauty of Sephora.
I'm trapped in your aura; this
must be the power of Pandora.
Dazed in this magical moment,
I'm aroused by the situation.
As I imagine all the ways of
various stimulation. The
Fahrenheit of fantasy rises
from this passionate energy.
I'm ready to make it a reality,
forever special in memory.
A few sexual innuendos.
A few sexual insinuations.
Then we let our bodies talk
and have deep conversations.
I want to approach you.
I can't pretend to be reluctant.

The power of that purple dress
is full of seduction.

I don't know if it's real
or painted on your skin.
It clings to your body gracefully
holding the pleasures within.

Your curves
are talking my language.
Your legs
walking in my language.
When you look into my eyes,
I can see your
thoughts in my language.

You have me distracted
I'm floating away!

I'm lost on your ocean
I'm floating away!

I'm touching the stars!
I'm floating away!

I'm passing the moon
in the outer of space……
……I've been stunned to
enchantment.

CINNAMON SWEAT

CINNAMON SWEAT

Sweet is code for cinnamon.
Sex is code for sweat
When you put them together,
you get, "cinnamon sweat".
Cinnamon sweat?
Yes, cinnamon sweat.
Hotness in the bed,
oh my, that cinnamon sweat!
The temperature is high
the energy is electric.
Full of erotic impulses
and the passion is kinetic.
Cinnamon sweat, enjoy
this invigorating intimacy.
And the savory satisfaction
from this fulfilling delicacy.
How sweet is good sex!
Oh, how sweet is good sex!
It's so sweet and wonderful
to have cinnamon sweat.

HER GENES IN BLUE JEANS

HER GENES
IN BLUE JEANS

A gray day & thunderstorms,
a gloomy day & rain drops.
Cloudy skies & murky seas,
even a blue champagne box.

These are my deepest thoughts,
about the color of
her blue jeans!

It's a swerving highway,
when eyes follow her curves.
A circling runway, nestling
her intimate hors d'oeuvres.

These are my deepest thoughts,
about the motion of
her blue jeans!

Covering her like paint.
Clinging to her like a magnet.
Stretching threads like magic,
turning denim to elastic.

These are my deepest thoughts,
about the fit of
her blue jeans!

I'm energized with a touch.
I'm mesmerized with a touch.
A hypnotic event when
caressing her with a touch.

These are my deepest thoughts,
about the feel of
her blue jeans!

SHE

KNOWS

IT

SHE KNOWS IT

She just wants somebody to sit with, in the hot tub with at the gym. Just to talk about the shallow parts of life, and the deep things within.
Her jade & crystal necklace lays over her shoulders, hanging gently on her chest. She wants you to notice the crystals, before you notice her breast. Then you can admire her creamy texture, as water water dances down her flesh. She has vast intellect, so pretty she glows. She has a figure that draws vigor, she's very witty so she knows. With every footstep her presence causes uproar. After she collects your attention and leaves, your eyes will want more.

Her body moves with jungle rhythm.... like a tribal beat.

And she knows it.

You'll adhere to her beauty, as if it was a seductive threat.

And she knows it.

Effortlessly, she'll lure you in with her naturally enticing & nonchalant traps.

And she knows it.

EGYPTIAN HONEY

EGYPTIAN HONEY

Are you made of Egyptian
honey, or dipped in exotic rum?
Your body is nectar for the
eyes, a juicy landscape under
a provocative sun. Warmth
radiates from your skin,
like a glowing hypnosis.
You have your own melody,
during moments of closeness.
It's a theme song that only the
heart can hear. There's
always thrilling thoughts of
desire and love, whenever you
are near. Time spent with you
is like a sentimental gift,
or a long walk on the pier.
You look like a combination of
Creo, with an Italian fancy.
With a combination of flavors,
caramel & pink taffy.

Such a rare find, like the
fine wine in a delicatessen.
It's hard to not catch feelings,
from being in your presence.
If you were standing in a
thunderstorm, your magical
complexion would still be
sunny. You illuminate with
golden passion; you must be
coated in Egyptian honey.

TIGER OF LOVE

TIGER OF LOVE

Love is a tiger that will eat you
alive. A nurturer and protector,
this is a balance that strives.
Seeming close as the
clouds with a promise of
elevation. Flowing through your
body as it penetrates your
imagination. Sunbathing in
love, until the sky gets dim.
When you make music over the
sunset, the stars twinkle from
within. Together is paradise
A mental connection
like a fantasy island.
Your heart never stops calling,
your heart never stops dialing.
Everlasting,
like a spiritual divinity.
Me, you, and love.
The passionate holy trinity.

Then calm as the sand
when it lays after a storm.
Inner twined body and mind,
together in cuddling form.
Dream, dream, dream,
whether asleep or awake.
Experiencing the joys of the
dream, as the actual physical
takes place.

DANCE FOR ME

DANCE FOR ME

DANCE FOR ME LOVE
  Move your body in that
motion. The fluidity of your
        movement………
  is a hypnotizing potion
DANCE FOR ME LOVE
  Bring down the ancient rains.
  Revolve and rotate slowly,
  as the earth does the same
DANCE FOR ME LOVE
  A magician with your hips
  What a pleasure to the eyes,
  a magic show when you grind
DANCE FOR ME LOVE
    With disco passion
    and exotic energy.
  Your body and your shadow,
    move to the beat with
      erotic synergy.

DANCE FOR ME LOVE
    The same way
 ocean waves groove.
I could be anywhere in the
 world….. but I'm here…..
   watching you move

DANCE FOR ME LOVE………..

THOUGHTLESS FEELINGS

THOUGHTLESS FEELINGS

Ice cream and candies, smooth wine and berries. Intimacy under the moonlight, will make moments intensely merry.

These are the things that go through your mind without even thinking....

Emotions in thought, become emotions in touch. Caressing the mind just a little, will caress the body very much.

These are the things that go through your mind without even thinking....

The flicker of the fireplace, rain drops on the window. The slow beat of the music brings a sensual tempo.

These are the things that go
through your mind without
even thinking....

From the luscious lips of a
candid kiss, to the paralleled
excitement of orgasmic bliss.
Our bodies intertwine,
softly grind & twist.
By the intensity of passion,
we know cupid didn't miss.
You feed the palate of my life,
you're such a delectable dish.

These are the things that go
through your mind without
even thinking....

EL-OH-VEE-E

EL-OH-VEE-E

Fill endless glasses with champagne. Let the love spill over the sides. Have a toast to emotions flying away. Tip your glass and watch them glide. Find a sandy beach, watch the water run past your ankles. Admire the beauty of the sunshine, let love leave you wrapped up and tangled. Frolic through your imagination and see what's meant for you. Find your perfect one for one, and become a perfect two. Love is in the air. Love is in the earths soil. Only love can freeze you in your tracks. And bring temperatures of passion to boil. The beautiful things in life are best shared with a loving companion.

How beautiful the sight to see, a heart as big as the Grand Canyon. Sweet scents to the nose, pretty pictures to the eyes. Tasty flavors to the tongue, blissful ecstasy to the mind. That's love, that is love, potent no matter the dosage. Protect its perfection like thorns and the roses.

GREY SPACE

GREY SPACE

Illumination radar!
Illumination radar!
Your presence illuminates and pops up all over my radar! The alarm is going crazy, you throw the system on the fritz. Once my eyes detected you, my brain became caught in a glitch.
I'm overwhelmed.
Thrown back.
My breathing has changed.
Is the earth flat? I must be going crazy! You looked at me as if I should be. I had thoughts of satisfying you. You looked at me as if I would be.
Your luscious body is pulsating, It's every man's favorite figure. You have a voluptuous display of curves, that intoxicates the eyes with sexual liquor.

There's a seriousness here.
You have an intimidating stare.
Someone could become a deer
in headlights. From being
caught in your glare. You want
to roughhouse and horseplay,
pillow fight and wrestle.
Now we're both out of breath,
hot, sweaty, and our
bodies locked in a nestle.
Then the horseplay turns to
four play, carnal urges, with an
appetite for pleasure.
As we move in sexual unison,
from the bed, to the wall,
to the dresser.
Grand finale on the couch,
climax, then roll over
on the floor.
Laying in grey space
falling asleep, wondering
when there'll be more.

THE COLORS OF ATTRACTION

THE COLORS OF ATTRACTION

On your body
Soft colors
Soft colors
Cotton candy and ice cream.
When I look at you, I see
cotton candy & ice cream

On your body
Soft colors
Soft colors
Everything about you is plush.
The sweet lips of your kiss,
will cause an adrenaline rush

The soft color of allure,
the urge for its embrace~
The soft color of your scent,
the yearning of its taste.

On your body
Bright colors
Bright colors
Sunshine and neon lights.
When I look at you
I see sunshine
And neon lights

On your body
Bright colors
Bright colors
Your energy electrifies.
The closer you get to me,
my energy intensifies.

The bright color of enticement, and the craving of your affection~ The bright color of excitement, and a body heat connection.

On your body
Soft colors
On your body
Bright colors
Whether its accessories
and clothes~ body paint
or radiant skin tones~
Soft colors or bright
colors~ your personality
just glows~

POUNCE

POUNCE..!!

It's the point when your urges become carnal. And you start craving the feel of skin against your skin, in sensuous positions.

Your inner jungle cat wants to pounce!

It's the point when your urges become tribal. And you feel the internal rhythmic beat of conga drums. Compelling you to thrust your body to the groove of another body

Your inner jungle cat wants to pounce!

It's the point when your urges
become animal like. And you
feel a passionate heat flow
through your body. Like mating
calls in the wild kingdom.

Your inner jungle cat wants to
pounce!

Intrigued by its thoughts,
seduced by its nature.
When sexual chemistry
is aroused, there is
no attraction greater

Your inner jungle cat wants to
pounce!

With those great curves,
body sculpture is admired.
With an appetite for vigor,
and a hunger for desire.

Your inner jungle cat wants to pounce!

Driven by its presence,
a shapely figure entices stare.
You want it right now,
with every breathe of the air.

Your inner jungle cat wants to pounce!

Pounce jungle cat! Pounce!

I BEAT THE LOVERS DRUM.........pt.2

I BEAT THE LOVERS DRUM pt. 2

LET ME ROCK YOU TO THE BEAT
LET ME MARINATE IN YOUR GROOVE

I COULD HIT IT HOW YOU LIKE IT
WITH ANY FLOW THAT YOU CHOOSE

LET ME TOUCH YOU ON YOUR RHYTHM
AND PLAY WITH YOUR VIBE

MY HANDS MOVE WITH THE TEMPO
THEY CARESS WHEN THEY GLIDE

I BEAT THE LOVERS DRUM

FAMILIAR FACES IN PLACES

FAMILIAR FACES IN PLACES

It was Saturday morning around 9:30am. I recognized this lawyer lady near a high-end coffee shop. She was standing at a busy intersection of a crowded crossing walk. She had on the smallest of shorts, a sports bra, and her long hair up in a pen. Through the slight hint of fog, is her beautifully vibrant skin. Maybe she's Caribbean. Maybe she's Indian. Somewhere in her melanin is the complexion of cinnamon. Maybe that's what's in her cup. Hot dolce to combat the morning chill. Pressed between her forearm and chest, is a tennis racket explaining her athletic build. Last time I seen her she was suited up on her way

into court. This time she's nearly naked on her way onto a court.
Her tranquilizing perfume is of nature in the meadows. Inhale one breath and be struck with cupid's arrow.
I decided to approach and engage.
Her subduing conversation is a treat. To my surprise when we talked, she said she recognized me .Not from where I seen her, but a whole other scene. From a mutual friend of friend birthday party, in Club Midnights VIP. As I started to recall my memory of the familiar event and think deeper. Wait! I think she was the one dressed up like a cheerleader......
Then it all started coming back. Halloween weekend out with my friend. Yeah that's right. I remember there was a girl dressed as cheerleader. She was dancing provocative in a dark corner. Alluringly drinking from her glass, as she wildly became one with the music.

*Men flocked to her and she flirted
magically with their every temptation.
I'm wowed by the mystery of her reality
I'm intimidated yet intrigued. This
conservative good girl has a wild side
indeed. She's a classy businesswoman by
day, under a naughty nightfall she plays.
When her sophisticated secrets,
are displayed in many ways.*

Never forget a face...

★
PROVOCATIVE
AFFIRMATIONS

★

IS

★

PROVOCATIVE AFFIRMATIONS

- *"I am the intrigue that leads to fantasy."*

- *"I can connect to sensual vibes."*

- *"My desire of love goes deeper than infatuation."*

- *"Look into me with those eyes and see your reflection in my mind."*

- *"I imagine love boats, drifting on a lazy rivers, and canoeing through a canal in Paris."*

- *"I know the midnight moon tells stories, of my utmost special memories".*

PROVOCATIVE AFFIRMATIONS

PROVOCATIVE AFFIRMATIONS

- *"I will speak love from the tongue, and let passion carry from my voice."*

- *"I need the temperature of body heat, from such a warm connection."*

- *"I want someone to count the stars in the sky and multiply them times my feelings and this infinite amount of love is why the earth has no ceiling."*

- *"I desire closeness like a shadow to a silhouette"*

- *"I will indulge myself in the body chemistry, embracing the moment is as taste the touch"*

PROVOCATIVE AFFIRMATIONS

- *"I can think provocatively and caress intimately."*

- *"I will find the treasure within the pleasure."*

- *"I know my enticing charisma is a conduit to the heart."*

- *"I will let my love flow powerfully."*

- *"I will romance the romantic and deliver passion to the passionate."*

- *"When I choose to honestly look, I can see the love of life in everything around me."*

PROVOCATIVE AFFIRMATIONS

- *"I will let my lovemaking lead the way."*

- *"My goal is to be a pleaser."*

- *"I will relax and let the mood take control."*

- *"I have the stamina for endless effort."*

- *"Seductively living in the moment, will make that moment a paradise."*

- *"I will use my body to translate and share every climax."*

- *"I'm sexy, passionate, and stir up emotions."*

PROVOCATIVE AFFIRMATIONS

- *"There's a treasure to be found at the end of an alluring trail."*

- *"I can use all my 5 senses on a romantic adventure."*

- *"My thought is to be fulfilling in every position."*

- *"This bedroom is a theme park and I'm the best ride."*

- *"I will enjoy every single second, and every single second will be enjoyed."*

- *"I take pleasure in giving pleasure first."*

- *"I will take it slow, and then change paces when it's time."*

PROVOCATIVE AFFIRMATIONS

PROVOCATIVE AFFIRMATIONS

- "Satisfaction is a must, so I will give it my all."

- "I'm excited and ready to indulge in desire."

- "I radiate intimacy and never let down."

- "Go with the flow of the chemistry and take it to new heights."

- "I will hug and hold on with erotic embrace."

- "I will make this a time, that will be wished to last forever."

- "Warm & wet kisses feel good."

PROVOCATIVE AFFIRMATIONS

PROVOCATIVE AFFIRMATIONS

- "I will be sensuously convincing like the power of good wine."

- "I will use whipped cream and strawberries to set the tone."

- "I am invigorating love."

- "I know my deepest of fantasies can be turned into pleasures."

- "My body will be the paint for the canvas of romance."

PROVOCATIVE AFFIRMATIONS

DEAR READER,
I hope you enjoyed..!!
Love always,

-*Cortez Maurell Lewis*

INSATIABLE SEDUCTIONS

www.ingramcontent.com/pod-product-compliance
Lightning Source LLC
Chambersburg PA
CBHW070544170426
43200CB00011B/2548